Tennis Unlimited

The Basic Elements of Sports Series

Tennis Unlimited

**By David J. O'Meara
and Ted J. Murray**

ICS BOOKS, Inc.

Merrillville, IN

To our fathers, Richard O'Meara
and James Murray

For more information on Tennis Unlimited programs
please use e-mail address *tennis.unlimited@pobox.com*

TENNIS UNLIMITED. THE BASIC ELEMENTS OF SPORTS SERIES
Copyright © 1997 by David J. O'Meara and Ted J. Murray
10 9 8 7 6 5 4 3 2 1

Printed in the U.S.A.

Published by:
ICS BOOKS, Inc
1370 E. 86th Place
Merrillville, IN 46410
800-541-7323

Library of Congress Cataloging-in-Publication Data

O'Meara, David J., 1963-
     Tennis Unlimited / by David J. O'Meara and Ted J. Murray.
        p. cm. — (The basic elements of sports series)
     Includes index.
     ISBN 1-57034-059-5
     1. Tennis—Training. 2. Tennis—Psychological aspects.
    I. Murray, Ted J., 1954- II. Title. III. Series : The basic elements
of sports series (Unnumbered)
GV1002.9.T705   1997   96-51750
796.342'2—dc21   CIP

Contents

Introduction

Tennis Unlimited is a simple, effective step-by-step process to improve your tennis game. It provides the framework for continuous growth toward your maximum potential. You will be taught uncomplicated skills—basic movements and body mechanics—which can be adapted to every situation in tennis. These natural movements allow your athletic ability to flow without excessive thinking. Tennis Unlimited will raise your level of play no matter what your age or ability.

Until now, most tennis instruction has focused exclusively on traditional tennis strokes, that must be hit from a perfect position. However, tennis is not just a beautiful stroke hit in the comfortable confines of a lesson. It is a game of constantly changing situations, which require different responses. This is the first book to explain clearly and logically the complete spectrum of tennis, *from Essential to Ideal*. The **Essentials** *are the vital elements of every shot in any situation*. The **Ideals** *use all sources of power when you do have time to get into perfect position*. Most tennis is played between these two extremes, which is why it is important to develop an entire range of options. Tennis Unlimited, with its pathway *from Essential to Ideal*, makes tennis more fun, more exciting, and more interesting for everyone, from the absolute beginner to the circuit player.

We have divided this book into three stages. STAGE 1 introduces the **Essentials** necessary to establish a feel for the ball, body, and racket.

STAGE 2 explains how the **Primary Shots** develop *from Essential to Ideal*. STAGE 3 describes how these primary shots adapt to handle the range of **Situations** encountered in tennis. Not everyone can become the number-one tennis player in the world because skill depends to some extent on a person's innate abilities. But if you strive to reach your own potential, you can become unlimited. Tennis Unlimited is your path to excellence. Anyone can swing a tennis racket, but you have the opportunity to be your best!

Each stage of the book opens with a section on the proper Mental Outlook that guides you to a state of mind conducive for your growth and enjoyment. Other sections heighten your Understanding of the mechanics of the sport; they teach you how to most proficiently hit a tennis ball in all circumstances. Finally, the sections on Skill Development offer individual exercises, drills, and challenging games designed to help you acquire a feel for what you are learning, while you have fun. As you practice these exercises, drills, and games, you will develop instincts, internalize skills, and create "muscle memory." Proper practice will soon allow you to respond and perform without consciously thinking about mechanics. You will develop terrific habits, which you can depend on throughout your life. There is an old Chinese proverb that emphasizes the importance of learning a new skill by experiencing it:

> *I hear and I forget.*
> *I see and I remember.*
> *I do and I understand.*

Our purpose in writing this book is to help you play better tennis. We do not want to overload you; we do not want to teach you unnecessary details. Instead, our mission is to guide you as you embark on an exciting path of discovery. Enjoy the process of Tennis Unlimited!

Stage 1: Essentials

MENTAL OUTLOOK
Making a Commitment to Growth

Tennis begins with the mind. Your mind can be your best friend or your worst enemy. An open mind welcomes change and seeks to improve, while a closed mind avoids change and wants to stay at status quo. Change is an integral part of growth. Your potential as an unlimited player lies in your willingness to learn and grow. If you have a desire to be truly unlimited, STAGE 1 sets you on the path to improvement.

STAGE 1 introduces you to the elements that are necessary to create every shot in Tennis Unlimited. As you work on these elements, called the essentials, you develop a feel for the ball. The essentials are

- Relating to the ball
- Preparing the racket
- Impacting the ball

Someone who is just learning to play tennis should concentrate on developing only these essentials. It does not make sense to worry about trying to hit actual shots until you have a good feel for the ball. If you have been playing tennis for some time, ask yourself whether or not you are comfortable with each of the essentials. Usually, it is a lack of comfort with the essentials that causes shots to fail during the various pressure situations faced in a tennis match. It is never too late to improve on the essentials. Although it is important to understand the essentials, it is even more important to gain a comfort with them by practicing the specific exercises that follow. If you are an experienced player, you may want to go directly to the challenging advanced drills, but time spent with the basic drills will improve your feel for the ball. By understanding and developing the essentials, the game of tennis will become easier and more enjoyable for you.

STAGE 1 is commonly overlooked in developing a player. Instructors usually jump into teaching the forehand and the backhand in initial lessons and bypass the essentials, but the essentials permeate every stage of a player's progression; they establish the solid foundation necessary to become an unlimited player. Therefore, they should not be passed over.

In the Skill Development portion of STAGE 1, you are asked to try several drills and exercises to enhance your feel for the essentials. Initially, your movements might feel uncomfortable and awkward, but perseverance will help you internalize the connection between ball, body, and racket. These drills and exercises are an important beginning to the formation of your "muscle memory."

Everyone has the ability to develop a sense of comfort with the tennis ball. Mental or physical ailments do not restrict an individual from enjoying the essentials of Tennis Unlimited. We have worked with pros, world-class juniors, club players, absolute beginners, wheelchair players, Paralympic participants, and the blind. All have been able to acquire the essentials. Some players, even after years of playing, thrive in tennis by using only the essentials.

It is up to you to make a commitment to growth. No one can do that for you. This commitment starts with the essentials. Your willingness to learn and grow is going to be your advantage over many players who are content with mediocrity. Unfortunately, many players see change as an arduous, lengthy, and unappealing ordeal. Because of this perception, these players can never reach their full potential. If you are willing to make a commitment to growth in your game, you will discover a wonderful, ongoing process that will build your confidence and will increase your enjoyment.

ESSENTIALS

UNDERSTANDING THE ESSENTIALS
Relating to the Ball

Developing a relationship to the ball means feeling comfortable with the path, bounce, and speed of the ball. It involves much more than simply watching the ball; it entails reading and reacting to your opponent's shot, moving to the ball, and positioning yourself effectively.

READ and REACT
Reading the situation begins when the ball is moving toward your opponent. Most players have been taught that watching the ball is the most important thing to concentrate on when playing tennis. Unfortunately, if you focus only on the ball, you miss out on valuable clues from your opponent. Your opponent's position and stance provide some information, but the racket tells you more. The speed of the swing, the angle of the racket, and the path of the follow-through reveal the spin, direction, length, and pace of the shot. By picking up these details when your opponent hits the ball, you can react immediately to meet the ball. With practice, you will learn to read your opponent's racket automatically, and you will be able to react instinctively. One bad habit that will prevent you from reacting instinctively is allowing the ball to bounce twice during practice. Make a commitment to try to reach every ball before the second bounce and you will be amazed at how many balls you retrieve.

MOVEMENT
There is no such thing as *the* perfect footwork pattern in tennis. Everyone moves differently, and every situation requires slightly different movements. A ball hit fairly close to you may require a couple of shuffle steps. A ball hit away from you may require a fast run. Running with your racket back slows you down and is unnatural. To achieve your greatest possible speed, pump your arms as well as your legs. A quick and powerful first step is most important, since it is often the difference between reaching a ball or not! The goal of movement is to reach the most comfortable position to hit your shot.

POSITIONING

After hitting a shot, you should move to the most effective court position to await your opponent's next shot. This location is usually in the middle of your opponent's possible shots. Diagrams 1a–c illustrate the layout of standard courts and the most effective court positioning for singles and doubles games.

DIAGRAM 1A

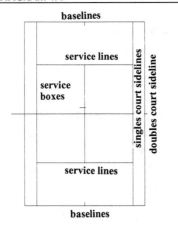

Preparing the racket

Your hands and wrists are essential in your preparation of the racket. Both hands work together on every shot. Your dominant hand is the bottom hand that grips the racket. Your non-dominant hand is the top hand that adjusts the racket.

The primary responsibility of the bottom hand is to grip the racket firmly enough to control it on every shot. The degree of firmness needed will vary with each shot. If you

DIAGRAM 1B

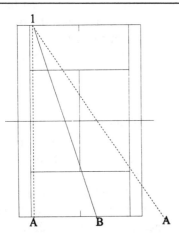

Lines A are the two extreme angles that an opponent can possibly hit from position 1. In singles, you should await the next shot anywhere along line B, which is in the center of your opponent's possible angles.

DIAGRAM 1C

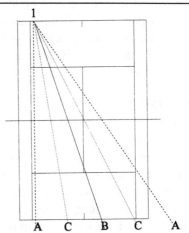

In doubles, the same concept applies, but partners should be positioned along lines C.
These are basic positions and can be modified according to your strengths and weaknesses as well as those of your opponents.

squeeze too tightly, you will not have the flexibility needed to produce a comfortable and powerful shot. Flexibility in the wrist is critical in Tennis Unlimited. Wrist acceleration increases racket speed, which is the primary source of power on all shots. A flexible wrist can also take pace off the ball and enable you to hit a variety of spins. The wrist is the key element in creatively controlling the power in modern rackets.

Your top hand will hold the racket up while you wait for the ball in your ready position. This enables the bottom hand to rest completely between shots and keeps the arm and shoulder relaxed, saving grip strength for the moment of impact. The top hand also helps prepare the racket, changes the grips when necessary, sets the angle of the racket, and grips the racket on two-handed shots.

Impacting the ball

The first two essentials prepare you for the moment of truth—the moment you impact the ball with the strings of your racket. Without impact, a beautifully executed swing is useless. There are many situations in a match where impact is all you need, especially when returning a hard hit ball.

Unfortunately, tennis lessons have often emphasized the phrase "take the racket back." This can lead to frustration, especially for people who have not yet developed eye-hand coordination. The only purpose of a backswing is to add power, yet there are more efficient ways of creating power than taking a big backswing. These power sources will be explained in STAGE 2 when we discuss ideal shots. Power is important in tennis, but it must be developed with control and consistency. You should focus on making impact with the ball on every shot. By concentrating on impact and the other essentials, you will have the foundation for a Tennis Unlimited game.

SKILL DEVELOPMENT FOR THE ESSENTIALS
Individual Exercises
BALL ON STRINGS
Purpose: To develop a feel for the ball on your strings.

Action: Place the ball in the middle of your strings, then walk or run while keeping the ball on the strings.

Advanced Variation: With the ball on your strings, turn your wrist and racket to the side until your racket is perpendicular to the ground, then quickly return the racket to its original position without dropping the ball. See how far you can turn the racket without dropping the ball. With practice, it is possible to turn the racket completely around without the ball leaving the strings.

BOUNCE UP
Purpose: To develop a sense of the ball impacting the strings.

Action: Hold your racket at waist level, with the strings and the palm of your hand facing up. Drop the ball into the center of the strings and bounce the ball up with minimal racket movement. See how many times you can bounce the ball up without missing.

Advanced Variations: After you've mastered the bounce up, try these three variations.

    1. Alternate bouncing the ball with palm up, then palm down.
    2. Bounce the ball up while walking or running.
    3. Bounce the ball up without focusing directly on the ball.

DRIBBLING
Purpose: To develop a basic feel for the ball hitting the strings.

Action: Dribble the ball on the ground with the racket.

Advanced Variations: These variations will give you a greater sense of the ball hitting the strings.

    1. Keep the racket below knee level the entire time.
    2. Alternate dribbling with the palm up and the palm down.
    3. Try to dribble using only the edge of the racket.
    4. Dribble while walking or running.
    5. Dribble without looking directly at the ball.

JUGGLING
Purpose: To develop a good feel for the ball, good eye-hand coordination, and improved ball placement on the serve.

Action: Start with one ball in your left hand. Lift it up to at least eye level and try to catch it with your right hand. Toss the ball back to your left hand. Do this until the actions are smooth, then add a second ball. The most important factor when adding the second ball is to develop a rhythmic pattern of alternating tosses. Once you master two balls, try three. Do not get discouraged; juggling is difficult to perfect. Time spent juggling on any level greatly enhances your comfort with the ball.

SUPER CATCH
Purpose: This is an advanced racket control drill to further develop a feel for the ball and a flexible wrist.

Action: Toss the ball up. Then try to catch it on the strings of your racket, letting the tip of the racket drop down as the ball descends. The goal is to catch the ball smoothly on the strings without bouncing. The higher you toss, the greater the challenge.

Advanced Variations: With a partner, try "super catching" back and forth from ten to fifteen feet apart.

Drills

TOSS and CATCH
Purpose: To develop a feel for the bounce of the ball.

DIAGRAM 1D

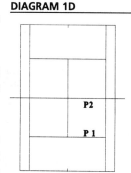

Location: Player 1 stands at the service line facing the net. Player 2 stands on the same side of the court near the net facing Player 1 (diagram 1d).

Action: Player 2 tosses the ball to various locations, short and deep and to both sides. Player 1 tries to catch every ball with both hands on one bounce.

PLAY CATCH
Purpose: To increase your comfort level with the ball, to better judge the flight and bounce of the ball, and to begin to understand strategy.

Location: Players stand on opposite service lines.

Action: Begin by tossing a ball back and forth across the net, catching the ball after one bounce. Set a goal for the number of consecutive catches you want to make, and meet your goal. Then, play catch for points. Players try to move each other around the service boxes, tossing the ball from one side to the other. Players must toss from the same place they catch the ball. A player wins a point if the opponent tosses the ball outside the service boxes or fails to catch the ball on the first bounce.

TWO BALL CHALLENGE

Purpose: To become comfortable catching balls in both hands, to learn to line up the ball, to develop vision skills, and to impact the ball with your strings.

Location: Player 1 stands at the service line facing the net. Player 2 stands on the same side of the court near the net facing Player 1 (diagram 1d).

Action: This is a multiple-step drill. Become comfortable with each step before proceeding to the next.

1. Both players become comfortable tossing and catching one ball with each hand.

2. Player 1 holds two balls in one hand, then tosses both balls simultaneously to Player 2. Player 2 tries to catch one ball in each hand. Player 2 tosses both balls back to Player 1 in the same manner.

3. Player 2 faces away from Player 1. Just after tossing both balls, Player 1 calls out Player 2's name. Player 2 then turns around and tries to catch both balls. Player 2 tosses both balls back to Player 1 in the same way.

4. Player 2 picks up a racket. Player 1 tosses both balls to Player 2. Player 2 taps one ball back to Player 1 with the racket while catching the second ball with the other hand. Try it! It is not as difficult as it seems. Player 1 continues tossing balls to Player 2 for several minutes, then the players switch positions.

5. Just after tossing the balls, Player 1 moves a few steps in any direction. Player 2 catches one ball and hits the other ball so that Player 1 can catch it. This exercise heightens simultaneous awareness of your opponent and the ball and teaches you to direct the ball to a specific target.

DEPTH PERCEPTION

Purpose: To develop a feel for the depth of balls coming to you by reading your opponent's racket.

Location: Player 1 stands at the service line across the net from Player 2. Player 2 stands just inside the baseline. The court is divided into three sections, as in diagram 1e.

Action: Player 1 hits a ball from the service line, and as soon as possible, Player 2 calls out the number of the area in which the ball will bounce. Player 2 also tries to return the ball on one bounce.

Advanced Variations: More experienced players hit the ball from the baseline initially, and both players call out the areas according to diagram 1f.

SHORT COURT

Purpose: To develop a feel for the ball and impact with the strings. To develop movement and strategy as well as control. This is a great warm-up for players at all levels.

Location: Players begin on opposite sides of the net at the service line (diagram 1g). Play is contained in the area between these service lines—an area called the short court.

Action: Players hit the ball softly back and forth, keeping it inside the service boxes. The key is to hit with minimal backswing focusing just on impact. There are a number of short court tennis drills that are very helpful. A couple of these are on the next page.

DIAGRAM 1E

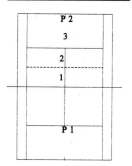

DIAGRAM 1F

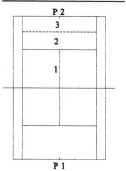

DIAGRAM 1G

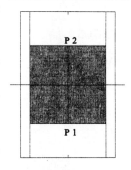

SHORT COURT UP and OVER

Purpose: To develop a feel for the ball and eliminate excessive backswing.

Action: Stop the incoming ball on your strings, so it pops up at your side. Let the ball bounce on the court, then hit it back over the net inside the service line.

Advanced Variations: As you stop the ball, direct it to the other side of your body and hit it back from that side.

TWO BALL SHORT COURT

Purpose: To develop peripheral vision and ball control.

Action: From opposite service lines, players hit each other a ball at the same time. Try to keep both balls going over the net as many times as possible. The goal is to control the balls in order to make it as simple as possible for each other. Both players should try to hit at the same time.

Advanced Variations: If you can hit fifteen or twenty balls in a row with two balls in play, try three balls. This is a real challenge! In this variation, one player starts each of the three balls, one at a time. It certainly makes it seem simple when you go back to hitting only one ball!

Games

DIAGRAM 1H

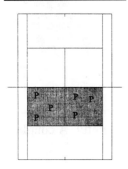

DRIBBLE TAG

Purpose: To develop your dribble, your vision, your quick movements, and to have fun.

Location: Anywhere from four to ten players stand inside the two service squares on the same side of the net (diagram 1h).

Action: All players must continuously dribble a ball with their rackets. One Player is *it* and tries to tag each of the other players with his or her free hand. Players are *out* if they are tagged or if they step outside the service boxes. Anyone who is *out* waits at the side of the court. One player remains *it* until all the other players are *out*. The last person *out* becomes *it* for the next round of the game.

SHORT COURT SINGLES
Purpose: To get a great workout and learn strategy in a controlled situation.

Action: Start each point by bouncing the ball and hitting it softly from the service line down the middle of the court. Every ball must be hit softly and must bounce once within the service box. Each player starts three points in a row. A player wins the point when the opponent fails to return the ball into the service box after one bounce. If the ball is not hit softly, play the point over. Play to seven or eleven points.

SHORT COURT DOUBLES
Action: Same court and rules as for Short Court Singles, but there are two players on each team, and teammates must alternate shots.

Stage 2:
Primary Shots

MENTAL OUTLOOK
Learning from Mistakes

Some people find tennis to be a very difficult sport to learn. Many beginners rapidly tire of picking up more tennis balls than they actually hit. Players achieve a level of competence, then stagnate, lacking the stimulation to reach new heights because they cannot get proper direction to help them attain the next level. In fact, the traditional manner of tennis instruction has served to limit people's ability to play the game, rather than to enhance their natural athletic talent.

Traditional tennis teaching is based on classic form: take the racket back early, turn sideways, step forward, hit with a sweeping stroke with the follow-through pointing forward, and, of course, always keep your eye on the ball. Unfortunately, most people are still being taught in the traditional manner. If you have been taught to play tennis this way, then you know what a shock it can be to go from a lesson to a match. The lovely strokes you learned in the lesson fall apart because your opponent seldom allows you to achieve the perfect position required for classical form. It's not your fault. You have simply been limited by the instructions that you were given.

Unlike the traditional approach, Tennis Unlimited deals with the reality of tennis as it provides fundamental concepts that actually work in match play. In a match, there is an opponent trying to make you uncomfortable. The *essential to ideal* approach allows you the freedom to effectively respond to your opponent, while it also provides you with the skills to gain control of the point. STAGE 2 explains the three primary shots in tennis: the volley, the return of serve, and the serve. In Tennis Unlimited, all shots in the game stem from these basic movements. You will be able to hit an effective shot whether you are in perfect position or not. This is the joy of the *essential to ideal* format!

Each of the primary shots requires the ability to create spin in order to progress from the *essential to ideal*. With powerful racket technology speeding up the game, spin is necessary to control the ball. We will teach you how to hit each type of spin later in this stage, but first it is important to understand the advantages of using spin as opposed to hitting flat:

- Spin allows you to hit the ball harder and still maintain control.

- Spin enables you to handle low balls more effectively. While lifting the ball up and over the net, spin brings the ball down quickly.

- Spin enables you to vary the net clearance, placement, and speed of your shots.

When you start learning spin or any new skill in Tennis Unlimited, you will make mistakes. It is part of the process of your development. Only through mistakes can you grow and improve. Having the perception that mistakes are good helps you prepare for a tennis match. A tennis match is filled with mistakes. Mistakes are intrinsic to the sport. If you fear hitting a tennis ball out or approaching the net, your growth will stagnate as you become one of the many limited tennis players who fear mistakes.

Tennis is one of the most forgiving sports. A tennis match has no time constraints, two serves, and a scoring system that allows for comebacks at any time. A tennis match is a forum in which you are allowed time to learn, to acquire direction, and to attain feedback that cannot always be gained at a practice session. Other sports also leave room for mistakes. Baseball has three strikes. Basketball has five fouls. Mistakes are an accepted part of sports and give you an opportunity to learn, adjust, and change. Take time to stop and reflect on what has occurred. Instead of dwelling on the fact that you made a mistake, realize the need for corrections and focus on the next point. If you see mistakes as opportunities to learn and improve, you will have no reason to fear or avoid mistakes. Mistakes will be the stepping stones on your way to heightened awareness as you enjoy your good shots, as well as your mistakes.

STAGE 2 allows you the opportunity to understand the primary shots of Tennis Unlimited and to experiment with them. We guarantee that mistakes will happen, and we hope you have fun learning from them.

VOLLEY

UNDERSTANDING THE VOLLEY

A volley is hitting the ball before it bounces. Most volleys are hit when a player is close to the net, but an unlimited player can volley from anywhere on the court.

ESSENTIALS
Relating to the Ball

Since you often are closer to the net when volleying, it is imperative that you quickly read and react to your opponent's shot. The action speeds up as you approach your opponent. Determine immediately whether your opponent is hitting a passing shot away from you, a lob over you, or a shot right at you. To react quickly to any of these options, assume a balanced ready position (figure 2-1) with your heels off the ground and the tip of your racket pointing forward. Your elbows are slightly bent and in front of your stomach. This allows you to move your racket as quickly as possible.

Preparing the Racket

The essential motion on the volley is setting the racket in front with the hands. The only movement should be wrist flexion, which points the strings forward with the bottom edge of the racket leading. Figure 2-2 shows proper preparation for a forehand volley and figure 2-3 shows preparation

FIGURE 2–1

Right

Left

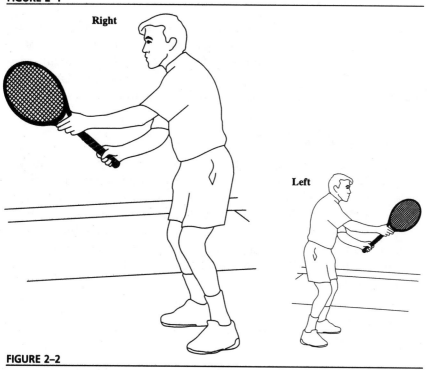

FIGURE 2–2

Right

Left

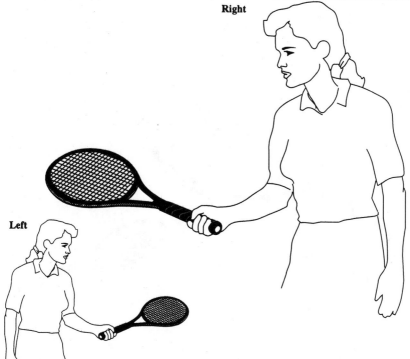

for a backhand volley. The most common mistake on the volley is taking the racket back. If you do not keep the racket in your field of vision at all times, you have taken it too far back. In order to get the maximum speed and full range of motion of the wrist, the hands must be relaxed. This preparation allows you to hit any type of volley in front of your body.

Impacting the Ball

At impact, your fingers squeeze the racket handle while your wrist moves forward. This causes the bottom edge of your racket to accelerate forward with your wrist and racket staying together. Finish with your strings pointing to the target. Figure 2-4 shows forehand volley finish and figure 2-5 shows backhand volley finish. The acceleration of the bottom edge enables you to hit a penetrating volley even when you are stretched out wide or returning a soft ball. This motion creates underspin, which is vital for an unlimited volley.

FIGURE 2–3

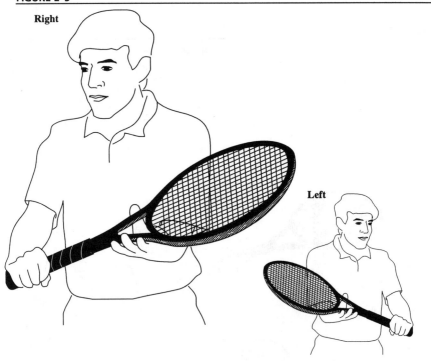

Right

Left

FIGURE 2–4

Right

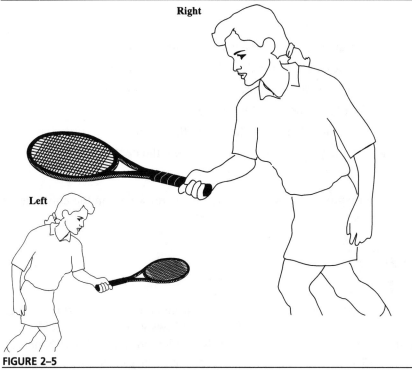

Left

FIGURE 2–5

Right

Left

Underspin helps you to:

- Get the ball over the net with minimal effort
- Control a hard hit ball and prevent it from sailing out
- Keep the ball low, forcing your opponent to hit up
- Hit drop volleys and lob volleys
- Volley low balls over the net with control
- Hit sharper angles while controlling the depth
- Volley aggressively even while moving forward

Underspin allows you to volley from anywhere on the court and is the trademark of an unlimited volleyer.

IDEALS

Grip

The ideal grip for the volley is the continental grip, sometimes called the hammer grip (figure 2-6). This grip allows you to move quickly with a strong wrist and an open racket for underspin on both forehand and backhand volleys without the need to change grips. There is actually no reason to change grips even if you have the time to do so. Once you understand that underspin is necessary for an effective volley, changing grips in order to hit a flat volley is no longer a desired option. Changing grips is one of the most difficult habits to break and prevents you from excelling at high-speed doubles or becoming an unlimited volleyer.

Backhand Volley: One Hand or Two?

A one-handed backhand volley is the ideal, even for someone with a two-handed backhand ground stroke. A two-handed backhand volley may be necessary for players who lack strength, but volleying with both hands inhibits the range of motion needed to protect your body and limits your reach on wide balls. If you must use both hands, learn to release the top hand when the ball is at your body or out wide. The goal in Tennis Unlimited is to develop enough strength to use a one-handed backhand volley exclusively. In hitting a one-handed backhand volley, your top hand still plays a major role. It helps your wrist set the racket quickly and prevents a backswing. For maximum strength, try to keep your top hand on the racket shaft up until impact. Proper use of your top hand ensures the greatest racket control without the limitations of a two-handed backhand.

Diagonal Power

Whenever possible, your legs should thrust diagonally toward the ball. The leg on the same side that you hit the volley pushes diagonally,

FIGURE 2–6

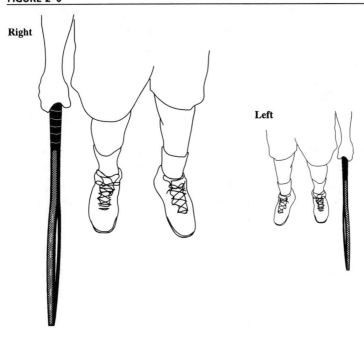

causing the opposite leg and shoulder to move to the ball. Figure 2-7 shows proper thrust on a forehand shot and figure 2-8 shows thrust on a backhand. This action adds power to the volley while creating better angles as you move closer to the net. The ideal volley utilizes perfect timing of the shoulders and legs with the acceleration of the bottom edge of the racket to generate optimum pace.

SKILL DEVELOPMENT FOR THE VOLLEY

Individual Exercises

UNDERSPIN UP
Purpose: To develop a feel for creating underspin with the wrist and racket.
Action: Bounce the ball on your racket strings creating underspin by moving the wrist forward and leading with the bottom edge. First, hit with your palm up, then try it with your knuckles up. Once you can do both, have fun alternating between the two sides.

BOUNCE TO EDGE
Purpose: To develop eye–hand coordination and quick racket reactions.

Action: Bounce the ball on the strings without underspin. Then, bounce it off the top edge of the racket. See how long you can alternate one hit on the strings and one hit on the edge. When you lose control off the edge, do not give up, but try to save it in any way possible without letting it hit the ground.

VOLLEYWALL
Purpose: To develop a solid, compact volley while strengthening your forearm.

Action: Using a hitting wall is a tremendous way to improve your volley. Practice as follows:

1. Start three feet from the wall. See how many forehand volleys you can hit in a row. To accomplish this, you need to lead with the bottom edge of the racket and use a very compact motion. Too much swing will cause the ball to fly past you and closing the racket will send the ball to your feet. After resting your arm, try the backhand volley. There is not sufficient time to grasp the racket completely with the top hand between every shot, but at least try to touch it.

FIGURE 2–7

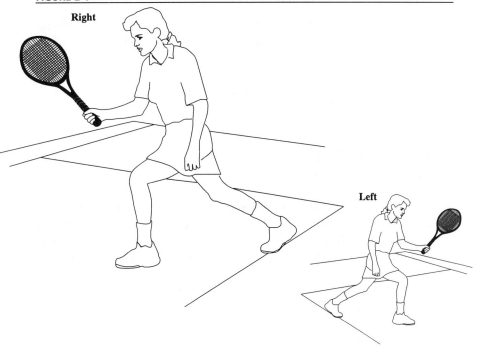

Right

Left

FIGURE 2–8

Right

Left

2. Move back another three feet from the wall and vary hitting forehand and backhand volleys. This develops quick reactions to set the wrist and racket.
3. Move to about ten feet from the wall. Keep moving your feet and bending your knees. You will get a tremendous workout!

Drills

UP AND OVER VOLLEY
Purpose: To develop a feel for working the bottom edge of the racket.

Action: Both players stand on opposite sides of the net, halfway between the service line and the net. Player 1 tosses underhand to Player 2. Player 2 first bounces the ball up with the strings, then volleys it back so Player 1 can catch it. Both the up and over are hit with underspin. Switch positions.

Advanced Variation: Once both players can control the up and over, both players use rackets to keep the Up and Over Volley going back and forth as long as possible. For even more of a challenge, try bouncing the ball up on the forehand side and volleying it over with the backhand or vice versa.

BACKHAND CATCH
Purpose: To develop the use of the top hand on the backhand volley.

Action: Player 1 is the hitter. Player 2 is the tosser. Player 1 holds the racket so the shaft of the racket rests on the wrist of the top hand. Player 2 tosses the ball and Player 1 tries to catch the toss with the top hand, keeping the wrist and shaft together (Figure 2-9). Player 2 gives a variety of tosses (especially low, wide balls) to force Player 1 to move. After a minute or so of catching, Player 1 then grasps the shaft of the racket with the top hand. The top hand remains on the shaft prior to impact, then is released and the bottom hand completes the volley. Think of catching with the top hand until the racket moves forward to volley.

WRIST ONLY
Purpose: To develop a feel for flexing only the wrist to prepare the racket on the volley.

Action: Player 1 is the hitter. Player 2 is the tosser. Players stand on opposite sides of the net, halfway between the net and service line. Player 1 faces forward placing the elbow of the top hand in front of the stomach and grabs the wrist of the bottom hand (figure 2-10). Player 2 alternates simple

FIGURE 2–9

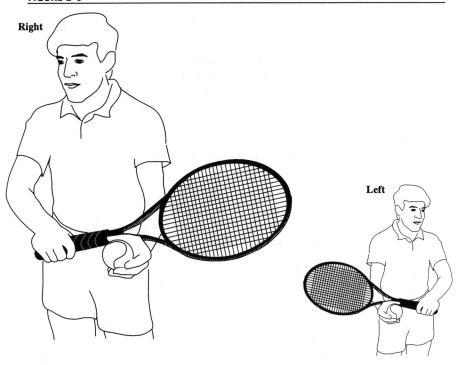

Right

Left

FIGURE 2–10

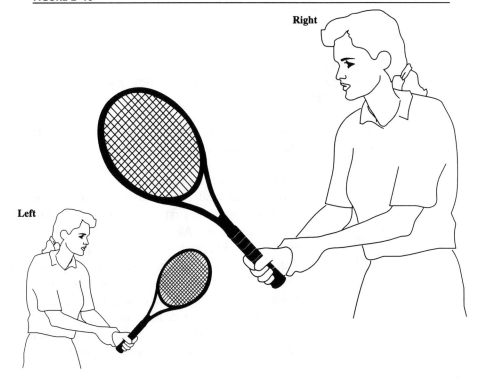

Right

Left

tosses to the forehand and backhand. The only part of the body Player 1 can move is the wrist (figure 2-11 shows movement for a forehand, and figure 2-12 shows movement for a backhand). Player 1 tries to return the ball so Player 2 can catch it. Once Player 1 can do this well, then Player 2 tosses balls randomly to the forehand or backhand. This forces Player 1 to react and set the racket with the wrist.

HIT and HOP
Purpose: To develop wrist and racket control on the volley when off balance.

Action: Both players are close to the net and must hop on one foot while volleying back and forth. See how many balls can you can hit back and forth in a row. You may switch legs when you get tired.

SERVICE LINE VOLLEYS
Purpose: To develop a consistent, deep volley.

Action: Both players must keep at least one foot behind the service line at all times. Volley back and forth for two minutes. Count how many volleys you can hit as a team in two minutes. Do not count any balls that bounce.

Games

MINI-VOLLEY GAME
Purpose: To develop touch and control on the volley. Excellent warm-up, especially for doubles.

Location: Down-the-line service boxes including alleys (diagram 2a). Player 1 starts at the service line. Player 2 stands closer to net.

DIAGRAM 2A

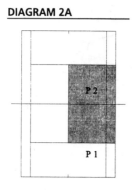

Action: Player 1 must let every ball bounce. Player 2 must hit every ball in the air. Either player can start the first point with an easy ball to the other player. Alternate starters throughout the game. Every ball must be hit softly, including overheads. The goal is to move the ball around and force each other into difficulty. A point is scored by a player when the opposite player hits a ball too hard or hits it out of bounds. Play a game to seven points. Then switch positions and play a second game.

FIGURE 2–11

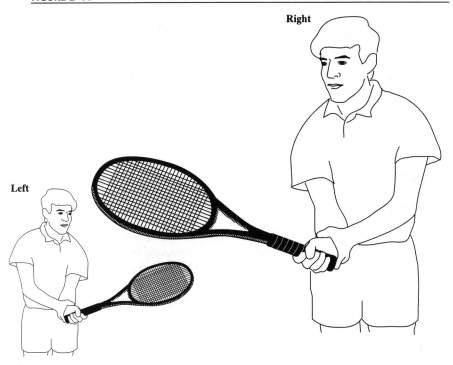

FIGURE 2–12

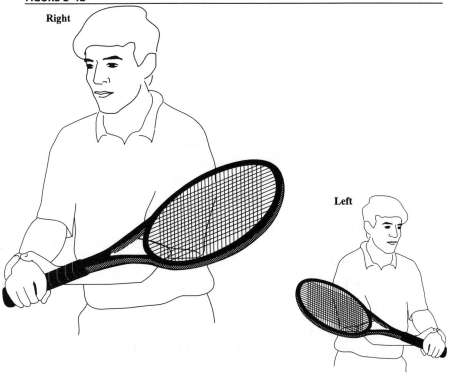

RETURN OF SERVE

UNDERSTANDING THE RETURN OF SERVE

Since it is attempted on every point, the return of serve is the second most important shot in tennis. It is also the foundation of all shots hit after the ball bounces.

ESSENTIALS

Relating to the Ball

Reading and reacting to a quality serve is one of the greatest challenges in tennis. You need to judge the direction, speed, spin, and bounce of the serve. You can pick up helpful tips from your opponent's toss, position, and serving tendencies. In order to react as quickly as possible, your ready position should be balanced with active feet and relaxed hands (figure 2-13).

Preparing the Racket

The initial movement is preparing the racket at your side. Both hands should be relaxed and able to work to control the racket. The top hand sets the racket edge while the bottom hand remains passive. Nothing is more limiting on the return of serve than the concept of "racket back." This hurts your timing, hinders your feel for the racket angle, and prevents you from adjusting to the incoming ball.

Impacting the Ball

The purpose of preparing the racket at your side is to consistently impact the ball in front of your body. Unlimited returners understand the significance of creating spin at impact. Both underspin and topspin are necessary to respond effectively to the variety of incoming serves.

Underspin is generally considered the defensive spin as well as the touch spin because it can be produced with very little racket motion. The ingredients for hitting quality underspin are

- A slightly open racket (bottom edge leading)
- The wrist and racket moving forward (not down)

The follow-through for underspin is out in front with the bottom edge of the racket pointing to your target. Figure 2-14 illustrates a forehand return

FIGURE 2–13

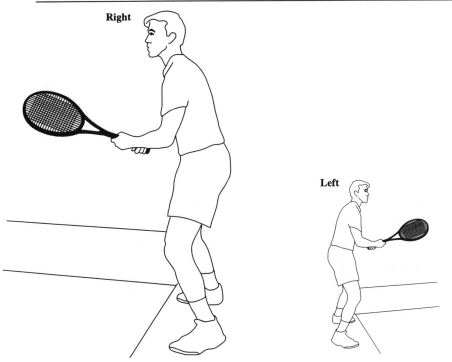

Right

Left

FIGURE 2–14

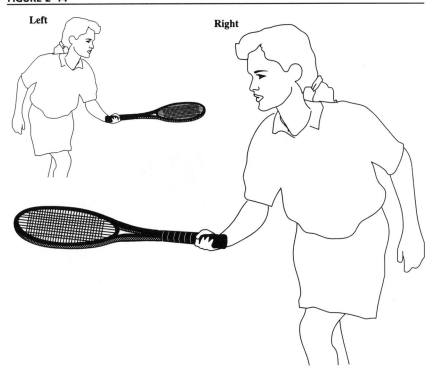

Left

Right

with underspin, and figure 2-15 illustrates a backhand return with underspin.

Underspin allows you to

- Block back difficult balls
- Hit balls that stay low after the bounce
- Hit softly with control

Topspin is the power spin because it enables you to hit the ball hard with control. Topspin is a forward spin that causes the ball to dip quickly and then bounce forward and up. The three ingredients of topspin are

- Low-to-high racket motion
- A closed racket (the top edge of the racket is leading)
- The wrist accelerating up and forward

You begin the topspin acceleration with the tip of the racket. The tremendous racket speed and the low-to-high motion cause the racket to finish over your opposite shoulder on the forehand (figure 2-16) and two-handed backhand (figure 2-17). If you try to stop the racket out in front

FIGURE 2–15

Right

Left

FIGURE 2–16

Right

Left

FIGURE 2–17

Right

Left

of you, your wrist slows down at impact, decreasing power and topspin. On a one-handed topspin backhand return, the racket finishes above the lead shoulder (figure 2-18).

Topspin allows you to hit

- Higher over the net
- Hard balls with control
- Sharply angled shots
- Deep, high-bouncing balls
- Balls that dip to a volleyer's feet

Topspin is the preferred spin on the majority of returns because of its offensive nature, but you also must have the ability to use underspin. Underspin enables you to return the most difficult serves and to keep your opponent off-balance.

IDEAL

Grips

There is not one ideal grip for the return of serve. The ideal grip on an underspin return is the same as on the volley, the continental grip. There are a range of grips that are effective in producing topspin. The purpose of the grip for a topspin return is to create a closed racket with the wrist in a strong and comfortable position (figure 2-19 shows a closed racket). A closed racket enables you to hit hard, driving topspin with total confidence. By leading with the top edge of the racket, you can achieve maximum forward acceleration of the racket and still keep the ball in the court.

Backhand Return of Serve: One Hand or Two?

Both one-handed and two-handed backhand returns are capable of hitting topspin well. A two-handed backhand return gives you the ability to hit a higher percentage of topspin backhands because your top hand provides greater strength on the return of serve. This additional strength also allows for better directional disguise, as your wrists allow changes in the shot just before impact. Many young players begin with the two-handed backhand return because the extra hand helps control the racket and adds power.

A one-handed backhand return provides you with better reach and the potential for greater variety than a two-handed backhand return.

FIGURE 2–18

Right

Left

FIGURE 2–19

Right

Left

However, it is more difficult to hit topspin when in trouble. This is why you see players with one-handed backhand returns hit underspin more often than two-handed players.

To be an unlimited returner, a two-handed backhand player must learn and practice a one-handed, underspin backhand, while a one-handed backhand player must be able to hit a strong topspin return. The choice between a backhand return with one or two hands is yours.

Diagonal Power

Traditional tennis has taught that ideal returns are hit by turning sideways and stepping into the ball with a closed stance (figure 2-20). Other coaches feel that an open stance with the feet parallel to the net is the ideal (figure 2-21). Unlimited returners use both closed and open stances, but not in an ideal situation. The ideal topspin return is hit from a stance between these two extremes called the diagonal stance. Figure 2-22 and

FIGURE 2–20

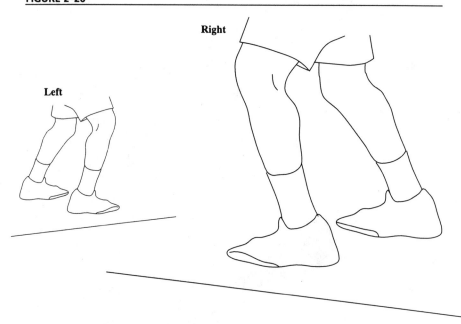

Right

Left

FIGURE 2–21

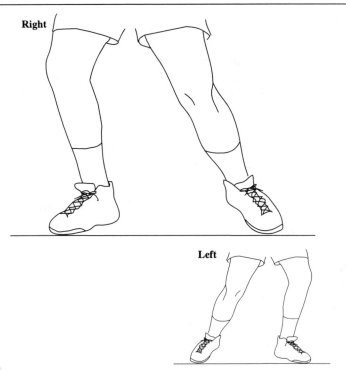

FIGURE 2–22

2-23 illustrate the proper diagonal stances for forehand and backhand returns with topspin. The diagonal stance is created from the ready position by turning the hips and shoulders during preparation. This shifts your weight to the back foot, while you use the front foot for stability. As your wrist begins to accelerate the racket, your hips and shoulders rotate as your back foot simultaneously pushes forward. The rotational thrust causes the racket to achieve optimum velocity and is often so forceful that you leave the ground. Figures 2-24 and 2-25 illustrate the completion of forehand and backhand returns.

SKILL DEVELOPMENT FOR THE RETURN OF SERVE

Individual Exercises

LOW TO HIGH

Purpose: To establish a feel for hitting topspin with no backswing.

Action: Kneel down with your knees at a 90-degree angle. Start with your racket touching the ground beside you, then drop the ball in front of you. Try to lift the ball over the net with your racket, swinging low to high on your forehand and backhand sides.

FIGURE 2–23

Right

Left

FIGURE 2–24

Right

Left

FIGURE 2–25

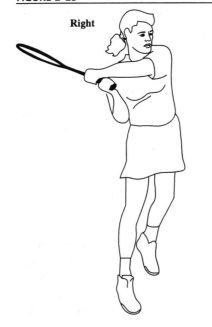

Right

Left

Drills

STOP and TOP
Purpose: To develop a feel for topspin.

Action: Player 1 and Player 2 stand just behind their respective service lines on each side of the court. Player 1 hits the ball so it bounces to Player 2. Player 2 pops the ball up. This is done by leading with the bottom edge of the racket to create underspin. After the ball bounces again, Player 2 lifts the ball back over the net with topspin to Player 1. Accelerate the wrist to create enough topspin to keep the ball inside the service line. Player 1 repeats the same action as Player 2 and they try to maintain a rally.

ALTERNATE SPINS
Purpose: To practice creating both topspin and underspin.

Action: Player 1 and Player 2 stand just behind their respective service lines on each side of the court. Player 1 hits only topspin and Player 2 hits only underspin. Always try to keep the ball inside the service lines. Switch spins after establishing a feel for the spin.

READING SPIN
Purpose: To learn to watch the opponent's racket to gain awareness of the spin being created and to learn to hit a variety of spins.

Location: Both players start at the baseline using the singles court.

Action: Player 1 hits every ball with spin, either topspin or underspin. Player 2 watches Player 1's racket and calls out as soon as possible which spin Player 1 is hitting. Player 2 tries to return every ball on the first bounce. Switch roles.

FORCEFUL FOREHAND RETURNS
Purpose: To develop a feel for hitting an aggressive return.

Action: Player 1 hits a high, short serve to Player 2 who is standing just behind the service line holding the racket closed, using only the top hand to hold the racket (the bottom hand is completely removed from the racket) (figure 2-26). After the ball bounces, Player 2 grips the racket with the bottom hand and drives the ball to a target near the baseline of Player 1. The acceleration of the racket should be forward and not upward. If the ball flies long, close the racket more with the top hand. If the ball hits the net, drive the racket more forward to the target.

FIGURE 2–26

Right

Left

Games

360 DEGREES

Purpose: To decrease the backswing of an inconsistent returner.

Location: Player 1 stands at the baseline prepared to serve. Player 2 is in ready position to return serve from the opposite baseline (diagram 2b).

Action: When Player 1 releases the ball toss on the serve, Player 2 turns completely around (360 degrees), then attempts to return the serve. Play out the point. Player 1 serves a game to five points. Then switch roles and play another game.

UP CLOSE and PERSONAL

Purpose: To practice returning difficult serves.

Location: Player 1 serves standing just behind the service line. Player 2 is ready to return serve from the opposite baseline (diagram 2c).

DIAGRAM 2B

DIAGRAM 2C

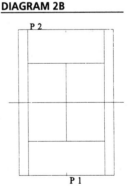

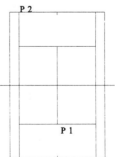

Action: Player 1 is allowed only one serve. If Player 1 misses the serve, Player 2 wins the point. If Player 2 returns the serve back into the court,

Player 2 wins the point. If Player 2 misses the return, Player 1 wins the point. Player 1 serves the entire game. The first player to reach seven points wins. Switch roles and play another game.

Advanced Variation: Once Player 2 starts to return the serve on a regular basis, play out the entire point. The first player to reach eleven wins the game.

RIP THE RETURN
Purpose: To hit an aggressive return of serve.

Location: Singles court

Action: Player 1 has only one serve. If Player 1 misses the serve, Player 2 wins the point. Player 2 tries to hit an aggressive return. Play out the point. If Player 2 hits a return winner that Player 1 cannot touch, Player 2 receives two points. Play to twenty-one points, switching servers every five points.

SERVE

UNDERSTANDING THE SERVE

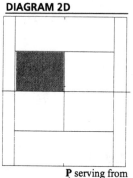

DIAGRAM 2D

P serving from
deuce court

DIAGRAM 2E

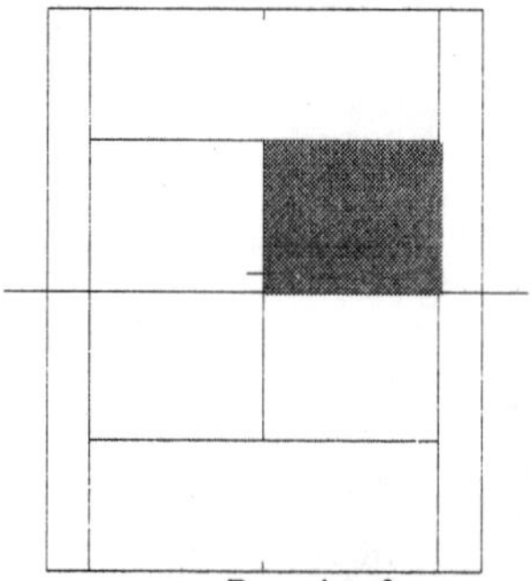

P serving from
Ad court

The serve starts every point. Thus, it is the most important shot in tennis. The first shot of each game is executed from behind the baseline and to the right of center and it is directed to the crosscourt service court (diagram 2d). If the first serve is not served inbounds, it is called a "fault," and a second is attempted from the same position. The serve for the second point of a game is directed to the other service court (diagram 2e). Again, one fault is allowed.

ESSENTIALS

Relating to the Ball

The serve is unique because it is the only shot in which you are not reacting to a ball hit to you by someone else. Therefore, you have total control of your relationship to the ball. The serve starts by tossing a ball to an area high enough to completely extend your arm and racket. You should not be dependent on a perfect toss in order to serve well, as the toss will vary slightly, especially when playing in wind or sun. The goal is to toss consistently within a range that allows you to serve comfortably.

Preparing the Racket

For beginners just developing a serve, start by using only your wrist. Begin with your racket hand by your ear with the wrist so loose that the racket tip drops down behind you. Toss the ball with your tossing hand and propel the racket up to the ball with a throwing motion.

For more advanced servers, a relaxed ready position is required to develop rhythm and timing. Relax your racket hand, wrist, and arm by supporting the racket with two or three fingers of the tossing hand (figure 2-27). From this ready position, the racket tip can drop freely and accelerate gradually as you toss the ball.

Impacting the Ball

Because there is no momentum from an incoming ball, you need a throwing motion to develop enough racket speed to hit the serve over the net. Your racket path goes upward at impact to provide the necessary net clearance. A flexible wrist allows you to adjust the angle of the strings to vary the serve placement and create spin.

FIGURE 2–27

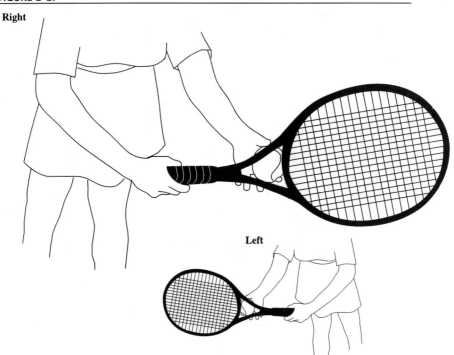

Right

Left

There are three types of serves: flat, slice, and topspin. If the strings point directly toward the net at impact, the serve is flat. If the strings strike the side of the ball, slice is created. If the racket tip starts below the ball and the strings move up and slightly across the ball, topspin is produced. Varying the toss may help exaggerate the spins (tossing to the side for slice, behind the head for topspin, and in front for a flat serve). However, relying on the toss to vary spin leads to inconsistency in the motion and rhythm of the serve and it tells the opponent what spin is coming. Disguising the spin and direction of the serve is crucial if you want to develop an ideal serve.

IDEALS
Grips

The ideal grip on the serve is the continental grip. This grip allows the most wrist flexibility to create the variety of spins. Any other grip makes it more difficult to hit all spins. If your goal is to develop an ideal serve, it is worthwhile to change gradually to a continental grip.

Diagonal Power

Power on the serve is achieved by acceleration of the racket tip. You can create some pace with the wrist alone if it is relaxed. If your grip is too tight, you limit your potential for power. The ideal serve uses the rest of the body to increase the acceleration of the racket.

There are two phases to gain supreme power. The first phase is the gathering phase, drawing together the parts of the body that contribute to a powerful serve. As your hands move upward, the gathering phase begins. Your front hip advances diagonally causing your shoulders to rotate. Your back shoulder lowers as your knees bend (figure 2-28).

The second phase is the launching phase, releasing energy from the gathered parts. As your wrist begins to accelerate the racket, your legs push against the ground driving your body up and out into the court at impact (figure 2-29).

It may take you some time to synchronize your body movements to develop the rhythm and timing required for your ultimate serve. Add only one movement at a time so you are not thinking of too many things when you serve. Remain as simple and relaxed as possible.

First and Second Serves

Increased net clearance and spin are the primary differences between the first and second serves. The first serve may be harder, flatter, and

FIGURE 2–28

Right

Left

FIGURE 2–29

Right

Left

closer to the net. On the second serve, you need a greater margin of error over the net for consistency; hitting up with topspin is a high percentage choice. Many people slow down their racket and rely on gravity to bring the second serve into the box. Although this may be appropriate at the beginning levels, it limits your ability to hit a quality second serve. The *only* difference between an ideal first and second serve is the angle of the racket to create more net clearance and spin.

SKILL DEVELOPMENT FOR THE SERVE

Individual Exercises

THROWING
Purpose: To develop a feel for the racket motion on the serve.

Action: Throw any type of ball in an overhand motion with your serving hand. A football, baseball, or tennis ball works well.

MIDAIR COLLISION
Purpose: To develop timing on the serve.

Action: Hold a tennis ball in each hand. Your serving hand holds its ball close to your ear. Your tossing hand tosses its ball up first. Then, your serving hand throws its ball at the other ball, trying to make the balls collide.

PENDULUM
Purpose: To develop a relaxed racket motion.

Action: Grip the racket with just your index finger, middle finger, and thumb of your bottom hand. Let the racket swing freely to form a pendulum at your side. The shoulders are relaxed to allow the racket to go up behind you. Gradually add the other fingers to the grip without squeezing tightly. Then, continue the pendulum to complete the full throwing motion, following through on the opposite side of your body. Listen for the sound of the racket accelerating. Try to increase the speed of the racket.

DRILLS

KNEELING SERVE
Purpose: To eliminate excessive foot motion and to emphasize hitting up.

Action: Serve with your back knee on the court. Also try to serve while sitting down.

WAY BACK
Purpose: To develop net clearance by hitting up.

Action: Serve from ten feet behind the baseline. Try to hit into the service box with enough arc to clear the net.

THE TOPSPIN TRAIL
Purpose: To develop a feel for the wrist motion on a topspin serve.

Action: Stand on the ad court side (deuce for a lefthander) with your body facing forward and both feet touching the baseline. Try to serve into the crosscourt doubles alley. If you need to create more topspin, start with the racket in front of your chest with your palm facing forward (figure 2-30).

FIGURE 2–30

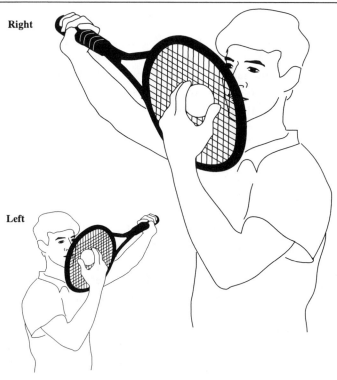

BOUNCE TO THE BACK

DIAGRAM 2F

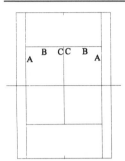

Purpose: To develop the ideal serve with driving topspin.

Action: Try to hit a topspin serve that bounces in the service box, then hits the back fence.

SPOT SERVING

Purpose: To train the wrist for directional control.

Action: Place three targets in each service box: A (Alley), B (Body), and C (Center). These are the locations you will serve toward during a match (diagram 2f). Choose a target (A, B, or C) and type of serve (flat, slice, or topspin) before hitting each serve. Mix and match targets and types of serves.

THUNDERBALL

Purpose: To develop wrist acceleration.

Action: Stand just behind the service line. Serve into the appropriate service box, seeing how fast you can serve by accelerating your wrist. This will help you increase the speed of your serve. When you go back to serving from behind the baseline, exaggerate the motion of hitting up. Otherwise, you will hit the first few serves into the net.

GAMES

SECOND SERVE CHALLENGE

Purpose: To gain confidence in your second serve.

DIAGRAM 2G

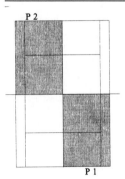

Action: On the singles court, Player 1 and Player 2 play one set. Only one serve is allowed on each point. The server will generally lose the first couple of games, but after an adjustment period, the server should start to win.

Advanced Variation: To practice for doubles, play crosscourt with doubles alleys included (diagram 2g). The server now is required to serve and volley.

Stage 3: Situations

MENTAL OUTLOOK
Achieving True Success

Tennis is a game of diverse situations. Sometimes you need to depend on the essentials, sometimes you can use the ideals, but most of the time, you are somewhere between the two extremes. This variety of situations is what makes tennis both challenging and fun. STAGE 3 takes you into match play and shows you how to adapt your shots to the situation. The quality of your opponent's shot and your skill level determine your situation. By correctly reading your opponent's shot, you become aware of the situation and can decide what response will be most effective. STAGE 3 reveals the four situations, ranging from *essential to ideal*, in Tennis Unlimited. We call them the four C's.

- Crisis Situation = You are in trouble, get the ball back into play
- Consistent Situation = Your opponent has hit a good shot, just be steady
- Creative Situation = The opportunity to keep your opponent off-balance by using a variety of shots
- Commanding Situation = An offensive position from which you can hit a forcing shot

Each situation requires a different response. During one single point in a game, you might find yourself in all four situations.

Your goal in playing Tennis Unlimited is to try to reach a commanding situation on every point. There are many times when you need to work through the other situations before achieving the ideal situation. Although you may not always be able to take command, your attempts to maximize each moment bring you nearer to your potential. Many limited players focus on the so-called big points. This state of mind prevents concentrated and sustained effort throughout the match. It shows that some players view winning, over which they have no control, as more important than their own effort to do their best on every point. For such players, their inability to control winning can be frustrating.

The reality of a tennis match is that someone always wins and someone always loses. This is innately true of sports. For too many people, enjoyment is in the result, rather than the process of playing. Competition can become a threat if you focus on the result and judge yourself in comparison to others. If you are happy only when you win, you often will be an unhappy person. Even the best of the best do not always win. Learn to revel in the ongoing process of tennis as you challenge yourself to be an unlimited player.

Winning and losing are just part of your journey in growth and learning. Try to focus your mind on the present moment and act without fear of the results. Mental toughness is the capacity to perform to the best of your ability at any given moment. Therefore, true success lies in how you try to achieve your goals. Success is not what you do; it is how you do it. That is what makes an unlimited player so special. That's what makes you shine!

STAGE 3 is your opportunity to excel in Tennis Unlimited. Have a great time adjusting to the ever-changing, ever-challenging situations of each point!

CRISIS

UNDERSTANDING CRISIS SITUATIONS

A crisis situation is a difficult spot to be in during a point. You are unbalanced, rushed, or unaware. You need something to rescue you and keep the point going. You want to find some way just to stay alive, to get the ball back over the net one more time. When you find yourself in a crisis situation, count on the essentials to save you. There are many tennis situations that require crisis management.

Difficult Returns of Serve

Situation: Your opponent hits a hard serve that puts you in trouble.

Response: Block the ball back with a slightly open racket.

Wide, Low Balls

Situation: You are reaching forward to get a drop shot or low ball, or you are stretching wide to retrieve a low ball.

Response: Isolate your wrist to hit underspin up for sufficient net clearance.

Balls Behind You

Situation: You are at the net and your opponent hits a deep lob over your head. As you turn and run after the ball, you need a shot to get the ball back into play.

Response: The sooner you get to the ball, the more options you will have. If the ball is still away from you, use only your hand and wrist to get the shot back over the net. Since you are trying to hit the ball in the opposite direction, too much arm movement on this shot slows down racket acceleration.

Fast Balls Hit at Any Part of the Body

Situation: Your opponent blasts a shot at your body when you are at the net.

Response: A backhand volley with a slightly open racket in front of your body protects you.

Half-volley

Situation: Your opponent hits a low shot and you cannot take the ball in the air to volley. You are forced to hit the ball on a short bounce—a shot called the half-volley. (A half-volley is not a volley because the ball is hit after it bounces; do not let the name trick you.)

Response: The *only* difference between a low volley and a half-volley, besides the bounce, is the angle of your racket. A low volley must have a very open racket to create enough arc to clear the net. A half-volley can be hit with the strings perpendicular to the ground, since the ball is bouncing up from the court and will rebound upward off the strings.

SKILL DEVELOPMENT FOR CRISIS SITUATIONS

Individual Exercise

911

Purpose: To practice rescuing balls that are hit behind you.

Action: Stand at the baseline facing the back fence. Drop a ball to the side of your body. Hit the ball over the net, using only your wrist for power.

Drills

CALL THE LOB

Purpose: To heighten awareness of where lobs will land in the court.

Action: Player 1 stands in front of the service line and hits a wide ball to Player 2. Player 2 lobs and calls out where the ball will land: "short," "good," or "long." Balls that land inside the service line are short, balls between the service line and baseline are good, and balls beyond the baseline are long.

Games

DIAGRAM 3A

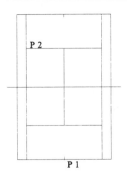

QUICK DECISION

Purpose: To develop quickness reading and reacting to the opponent's serve.

Location: Player 1 stands at the baseline prepared to serve. Player 2 stands just behind the service line ready to return the serve (diagram 3a).

Action: From this position, Player 2 is forced to execute difficult half-volleys to return the serve.

Player 2 wins the point for returning the ball back into the court. Player 1 wins the point when Player 2 fails to do this. The first player to reach eleven points wins.

Advanced Variation: If Player 2 is able to return the serve on a regular basis, continue to play the entire point. The first player to reach seven points wins.

CONSISTENCY

UNDERSTANDING CONSISTENT SITUATIONS

Consistency is a key element in becoming a good tennis player. With consistency alone, it is possible to be successful. Consistency alone does not make an unlimited player, but there are certain situations that call for a safe, solid shot.

Second Serve

Situation: You are hitting a second serve.

Response: Consistency is the basis of an intelligent second serve. It's nice to be creative on the second serve, but being consistent is more important. If you can hit the second serve deep in the box on a regular basis, you will gain confidence to be more aggressive on both your first and second serves.

Returning a Strong Serve

Situation: Your opponent hits a strong serve.

Response: Returning the ball down the middle is the safe response. If you try to get too creative returning a very good first serve, you may err. If you consistently return your opponent's best serves, your opponent often will try to serve harder or closer to the line, making more mistakes as the match progresses.

Deep Ground Strokes

Situation: Your opponent hits a deep ground stroke that bounces close to the baseline.

Response: When hitting from behind the baseline, you will have difficulty hitting sharp angles. Therefore, your best response is to try to hit deep with good net clearance.

Low Volley

Situation: You are coming in to the net and your opponent hits low to your feet.

Response: Volley deep with underspin. This gives you time to gain position for the next volley and gives the opponent less angle for a passing shot.

SKILL DEVELOPMENT FOR CONSISTENT SITUATIONS

Drills

CHANGING DIRECTION
Purpose: To practice hitting ground strokes down-the-line and crosscourt while on the move.

Action: Player 1 and Player 2 begin at the baseline. Player 1 must hit crosscourt and Player 2 must hit down-the-line. After a few minutes, Player 1 and Player 2 switch directions.

CONSECUTIVE HITS
Purpose: To develop consistency.

Action: Try to hit as many shots as possible without a miss. Count the number of times both players hit.

1. Inside the service boxes
2. In only one alley
3. Baseline to baseline in the singles court
4. Baseline to baseline crosscourt, including alleys
5. Beyond the service line

COOPERATIVE COMPETITION

Purpose: To work together to try to hit as many balls as possible in three minutes.

Location: Player 1 and Player 2 stand at opposite baselines down-the-line. Player 3 and Player 4 do the same thing on the other half of the court (diagram 3b).

Action: Player 1 and Player 2 are a team competing against Player 3 and Player 4. Each team tries to hit as many balls as possible back and forth in three minutes. The team that hits the most balls wins. Count only the balls that land beyond the service line. Variation: Play crosscourt.

Games

AFTER SIX

Purpose: To develop consistency in point play.

Action: Both Player 1 and Player 2 start at the baselines. The first ball is hit down the middle. Both players must hit the ball back and forth six times for the point to start. After the sixth shot, the point begins. The first player to reach ten points wins.

CREATIVITY

UNDERSTANDING CREATIVE SITUATIONS

A creative situation is a situation that is not determined by the opponent's shot. Creativity means using a variety of shot options to keep your opponent off-balance. It can lead to more mistakes than consistency, but it is necessary in order to progress to a higher level of tennis. Creativity is often necessary to gain control of a point.

Serve

The tennis serve is very similar to the baseball pitch. Great pitchers may not have the most incredible fast ball, but they constantly keep the batter off-balance, varying the speed, types, and location of pitches. Creative servers do the same thing; they vary the speed, spin, and placement of each serve. They are unpredictable and do not allow the receiver to get comfortable. Second serves also should be hit with some variety, even at the expense of an occasional double fault.

Return of Serve

When returning an average serve, you can be creative in varying your returns. Unless you are under pressure from an excellent serve, your goal is to try to take control of the point on the return of serve. It is helpful to have a target in mind prior to your opponent's serve, so you can be decisive with the return.

Set Up Shots

Set up shots are used in combination with other shots to take control of the point by opening up the court and making your opponent run. One of the best ways to move your opponent is by hitting sharp, crosscourt angles with topspin. These are referred to as side-t shots, since your target is the **T** formed by the service line and the sideline. A side-t is often hit following a deep shot that forces your opponent to hit shorter, giving you a better angle. Once you force your opponent outside the sidelines, you have gained control of the point.

Another way to make your opponent run is by hitting a drop shot. The drop shot should always be hit with underspin to keep the second bounce close to the first bounce. Underspin also creates the arc over the net which is necessary to land the first bounce as close to the net as possible. Obviously, the arc cannot be too high or it gives your opponent ample time to reach the ball. The perfect drop shot is disguised so your opponent cannot read it. It should look like a normal ground stroke until impact. At that point, the racket stops with the strings pointing upward, which creates exaggerated underspin. A similar shot is the drop volley. The characteristics are the same, except a great drop volley looks like a normal volley and requires softer hands to take the pace off the incoming ball. On the finish for a drop shot, the racket is open and the tip is dropping down (figure 3-1).

Set Up Shots against a Net Rusher

When the opponent is at the net, many players think they must blast a passing shot, regardless of the incoming ball. If you can use spin creatively, you have more than one option.

FIGURE 3–1

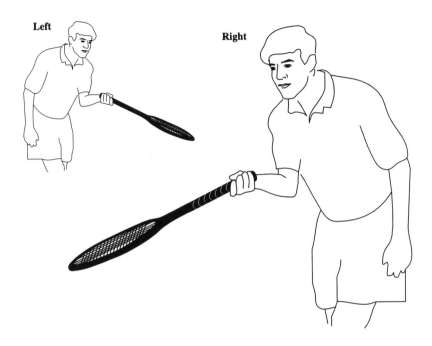

Left

Right

One of the most effective options is the use of topspin that drops the ball rapidly at your opponent's feet. Hit this shot by emphasizing your upward motion of the wrist and racket tip to create extra topspin. Dipping topspin forces your opponent to hit up, often giving you a chance to move in and take control.

If your opponent begins to move forward, you may choose to hit a topspin lob. The motion is the same as a regular topspin shot until you exaggerate the lifting motion of the arm and wrist at impact. If you pull up too abruptly, your lob will be short and will give the opponent an easy overhead.

When your opponent is at the net and hits a deep shot to the corner, it is still possible to be creative. The safest shot is the defensive underspin lob, which is hit high and deep. This forces your opponent away from the net. Another option is to hit a low, underspin shot, which is extremely effective, especially if your opponent has moved back expecting the lob. Your wrist accelerates forward to create penetrating underspin, which keeps the ball low.

Approaching the Net

If you are trying to control the point, you will look for opportunities to approach the net. In order to approach the net successfully, you must be creative.

The most aggressive way to reach the net is to serve and volley. By taking the first opportunity to come to the net, you are forcing your opponent to respond to you. Make the decision to serve and volley before serving, not after seeing the result of your serve. Your momentum into the net begins with the launching phase of the serve. Just before your opponent makes impact with the return, hesitate in a balanced ready position. This enables you to read and react immediately to your opponent's shot. If possible, try to move diagonally to the first volley. The serve and volley is a valuable option for singles and a necessity for unlimited doubles.

In doubles, you often want to come to the net as you return the serve. This is called the chip and charge. Make the decision to chip and charge prior to your opponent's serve. The value of the chip and charge is the ability to hit the return while moving forward. Think of it as a volley hit after the bounce. A continental grip is most effective because you want to hit the ball in front of you and create underspin as you move forward. The ideal shot is one that either stays low to the feet of your opponent or penetrates deep to force your opponent back. In doubles, the shot normally is hit crosscourt; whereas in singles, the preferred shot is hit down-the-line. The chip and charge can be very intimidating, especially to opponents who lack confidence in their second serve.

When your opponent hits a short ball, you can come to the net by hitting an approach shot. This is a transitional shot from the baseline to the net. In an approach shot, you move through impact. If you stop, you miss out on advancing to a more effective volley position. Continue forward until you establish a balanced ready position just prior to your opponent's shot.

Your decision on the type of spin to hit on an approach shot is based on the height of the ball when you make impact. Hitting underspin on an approach shot allows you to

- Hit on the run because it requires no backswing and little racket movement
- Hit balls at any height
- Vary the depth of your shot and keep the ball low

■ Disguise the shot because you can change the depth at the last moment

You can hit topspin for a more powerful approach shot, but it must be hit much more selectively than underspin because

■ It is more difficult to hit topspin on the run

■ Hitting hard can prevent you from reaching your best volleying position

■ It is difficult to hit topspin on low balls (though it is possible, using your wrist to exaggerate the lifting motion)

■ Your ball will bounce up, making it easier for your opponent to hit a passing shot

When you hit a shot that forces your opponent into a crisis situation, move a couple of steps inside the baseline. It is important to be in your ready position before your opponent hits the ball. If your opponent lobs the ball back, move in and hit an approach volley. This keeps your opponent on the defensive. Normally the approach volley is hit with underspin; however, a topspin approach volley can be very effective. If you take no backswing and use a fast wrist, the topspin approach volley can be a consistent, powerful reply.

SKILL DEVELOPMENT FOR CREATIVE SITUATIONS

Games

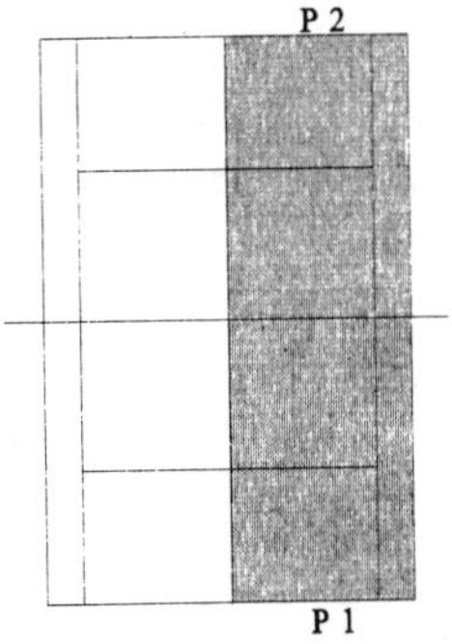

RUSH and CRUSH

Purpose: To learn to approach the net under a variety of conditions.

DIAGRAM 3C

Location: Half-court including the doubles alley. Player 1 and Player 2 begin each point at the baseline (diagram 3c).

Action: Player 1 starts the point by bouncing and hitting to any part of the opponent's half-court. Player 1 cannot move inside the baseline until Player 2 makes impact. Player 2 may come in at any time, but cannot volley the serve. The goal

DIAGRAM 3D

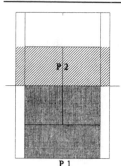

for both players is to get inside the service line. A point is awarded only if the player winning the point is inside the service line when the point ends. If neither player is inside the service line, no one gets a point. The first player to reach eleven points wins. Alternate serves every three points *played*. (Even if no point is scored, it counts as a point played.)

PASS ME IF YOU CAN!

Purpose: To practice angled, dipping passing shots.

Location: Player 1 is at the baseline. Player 2 is at the net. Player 1 must hit into the service boxes and adjacent alleys. Player 2 must hit into the singles court (diagram 3d).

Action: Player 2 starts the point by hitting an easy ball down the middle of the court. Player 1 tries to hit low, angled passing shots. First player to eleven wins the game.

Variation 1: If the baseline player starts winning easily, play a game without using the alleys.

Variation 2: If the net person is winning consistently, play a game whereby Player 1 can hit a lob behind the service line.

CHIP and CHARGE

Purpose: To practice chipping and charging on return of serve in doubles.

DIAGRAM 3E

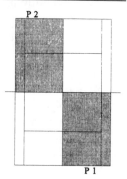

Location: Crosscourt half-court, including doubles alleys. Player 1 is serving. Player 2 is receiving serve (diagram 3e).

Action: Player 1 is allowed only one serve, with the option of serving and volleying or staying back. Player 2 must chip and charge on every serve. Play to seven points, (remaining on the same side of the court) and keeping the same server for the entire game. Switch servers for game two. Switch to the opposite half-court for games three and four. Play at least four games so both players serve and receive on both sides.

OPEN UP THE COURT

Purpose: To practice opening up the court and moving your opponent.

Location: Crosscourt half-court, including doubles alleys. Player 1 and Player 2 are at opposite baselines (diagram 3f).

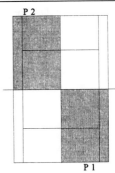

DIAGRAM 3F

Action: Either player starts the point by bouncing the ball and hitting crosscourt. Players must hit only forehands or only backhands the entire game. If both players agree to hit only forehands, then a player hitting a backhand automatically loses the point. Players 1 and 2 should try a variety of depths and angles to create an opening or force a mistake. The first player to reach eleven points wins the game.

FULL COURT FOREHANDS

Purpose: To develop footwork, strategy, and creativity on the forehand.

Location: Singles court. Player 1 and Player 2 are at opposite baselines.

Action: Either player hits a ball down the middle of the court to start the point. Both players try to move each other around the singles court, hitting only forehands. A player hitting a backhand automatically loses the point. Court coverage in this game is crucial. The first player to reach eleven points wins the game. For a real challenge, you also play this game with only backhands.

COMMANDING

UNDERSTANDING COMMANDING SITUATIONS

A commanding situation means you are in an ideal position. The goal of every point is to achieve a commanding situation. An unlimited player tries to make the most of an offensive opportunity by forcing the opponent into a difficult predicament.

First Serve

Situation: You are hitting a first serve.

Response: Try to take immediate control of the point by using a variety of targets, speeds, and spins.

Returning an Easy Serve

Situation: Your opponent hits a weak serve.

Response: Take control of the point by putting your opponent on the defensive with an ideal return of serve.

High Ground Stroke

Situation: Your opponent hits a short, high-bouncing ball, and you can move inside the baseline.

Response: Lead with the top edge of your racket and accelerate forward, hitting the top of the ball. As in the return of serve, utilize your diagonal power in this ideal situation. Since the ball is above net level, there is no reason for a low-to-high swing, as this will only take pace off the ball. If the ball flies long, close the racket more with your top hand. If the ball hits the net, drive the racket further forward.

High Volley

Situation: You are at the net and your opponent hits you a shoulder-high ball.

Response: Move diagonally to the ball to get the sharp crosscourt angles where most commanding volleys should be hit. The most common mistakes that players make on this shot are not moving diagonally with their feet and taking an excessive backswing.

Overhead Smash

Situation: You are at the net and your opponent hits a medium-deep lob.

Response: Try to hit the lob in the air with an overhead smash. The motion on the overhead is similar to the serve with emphasis on the wrist. The arm motion on the overhead is more compact than on the serve, since timing must be more precise. With your position close to the net, the overhead is hit flat for maximum power.

The first consideration in hitting an overhead is recognizing the lob and immediately turning sideways. Running back sideways (crossing the legs) is much faster than either backpedaling (without turning sideways) or shuffling sideways (without crossing the legs). Do not hesitate to jump up to hit the smash, as jumping can enable you to gain better reach, timing, and power.

SKILL DEVELOPMENT FOR COMMANDING SITUATIONS

Drills

TWO-MINUTE BLAST
Purpose: To practice accelerating and hitting hard without worrying about the result.

Action: Hitting baseline to baseline, Player 1 hits for two minutes straight, trying to hit with total power off every ball. Player 2 tries to be consistent and return as many balls as possible. Switch roles for another two minutes.

Games

CLOSE and CRANK
Purpose: To practice hitting commanding shots off high, midcourt balls.

Location: Singles court. Both players start at the baseline.

Action: Player 1 starts the point by hitting a short, high-bouncing ball that must land inside the service line. Player 2 moves in and tries to hit an ideal ground stroke with diagonal power. Play out the point. Player 2 receives a bonus point if Player 1 cannot touch the first shot. Player 1 receives a bonus point for returning the first shot. With the attacker and defender switching roles every five points, play to twenty-one points.

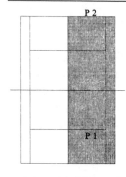

DIAGRAM 3G

UP and BACK

Purpose: To practice hitting volleys and overheads in a limited area.

Location: Half-court, including alleys. Player 1 starts at the service line. Player 2 starts at the baseline (diagram 3g).

Action: Player 1 starts the point by bouncing the ball and hitting an approach shot beyond the service line. Play out the point. Play a game to 5 points with Player 1 starting at the service line. Then play a second game with Player 2 starting at the service line. You can play additional games crosscourt.

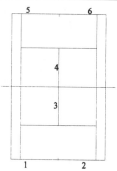

DIAGRAM 3H

POACHING GAME

Purpose: To practice diagonal movement in doubles when moving into your partner's side of the court to volley.

Location: Doubles court. Two teams of three players each. One player from each team is at the net and cannot move behind the service line. The other two players are at the baseline (diagram 3h).

Action: Player 1 starts the point by dropping a ball and hitting it off the bounce. No lobs are allowed. Player 1 starts the first three points, Player 2 the next three, Player 5 the next three and Player 6 the next three. Net players from both teams try to volley any ball they can reach. Play out each point. The winner is the first team to reach ten points. Play three games, rotating positions at the end of each game so that every player plays one game at the net.

SMASH AWAY

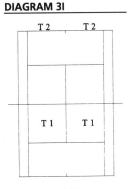

Purpose: To practice hitting commanding overheads.

Location: Two doubles teams using the doubles court. Team 1 starts inside service line and Team 2 starts at the baseline (diagram 3i).

Action: Team 2 starts each point by lobbing, alternating to a different player each point. Play out each point. Team 2 may come to the net if there is the opportunity. Play a game to ten points. Play a second game with Team 2 starting at the net and Team 1 at the baseline.

DOUBLES RUSH and CRUSH

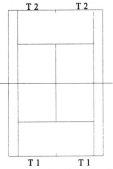

Purpose: To play aggressive doubles with all players coming to the net.

Location: Doubles court. Both doubles teams start each point at the baseline (diagram 3j).

Action: Team 1 starts by dropping a ball and hitting it off the bounce. The ball must land inside the service line. Team 2 has the first chance to approach the net. Team 1 cannot move inside the baseline until Team 2 hits the ball. In order to receive a point, both players from the winning team must be inside the service line when the point ends. Each player starts three points in a row, then the serve rotates among all four players. The winner is the first team to reach ten points.

Conclusion

You have reached the conclusion of this book. This is not the end, but rather a beginning. By learning the three Stages of Tennis Unlimited, you now have a blueprint for becoming an unlimited player. Tables 1 and 2 offer you two *essential to ideal* checklists, summarizing the blueprint.

TABLE 1. The Shots: From Essentials to Ideal

Work hard to build on your primary shots, progressing from the necessary (1) to the ideal (5).

The Shot	*The Progression from Essentials to Ideals*
Volley	1. Ready position 2. Wrist flexion 3. Continental grip 4. Underspin added 5. Diagonal movement
Return of Serve	1. Ready position 2. Top hand sets the grip 3. Racket to your side 4. Topspin or underspin added 5. Diagonal stance
Serve	1. Relaxed wrist 2. Toss within range 3. Continental grip 4. Gather and launch your serve 5. Alternate topspins, slices, and flat serves

TABLE 2. The Situations: From Essential to Ideal

Work hard to try and reach a commanding position during each point of each game you play.

The Situation	The Appropriate Response
Crisis	Use only essentials to get the ball back over the net
Consistency	Use net clearance to keep the ball deep
Creativity	Use variety to create spins and angles
Commanding	Use ideals to produce maximum power

The process of improving your tennis game entails much more than simply reading this book. It requires a commitment to act upon this knowledge by constantly trying to improve both your mental outlook and your physical skills. Becoming unlimited is a process that will challenge and stimulate you throughout your entire life. The fun and excitement come from experimenting with the exercises, drills, and games that are your building blocks of progress. Revel in your newly acquired freedom as you enjoy hitting a tennis ball in practice or in a match. Welcome to the wonderful world of Tennis Unlimited!

Index